CW01192577

Punk Faun: A Bar Rock Pastel

Punk Faun: A Bar Rock Pastel

redell olsen

SUBPRESS
OAKLAND

The author wishes to thank the editors of the publications in which this poem has been included and the organisers of the reading series and events at which this poem has been heard. Extracts and earlier versions of *Punk Faun: a baroque pastel* have previously appeared in: *Archive of The Now, Blackbox Manifold, Dusie, How(2), I'll Drown My Book, Conceptual Writing By Women* (Les Figues Press, 2012), *I.E.& P.R, Openned, Penn Sound, Pilot: A Journal of Contemporary Poetry, The Argotist, This Corner, Veer* and publications from: *Centre International de Poésie Marseille* (2006), *Cambridge Reading Series* (2010) and *The Second Annual Sussex Poetry Festival* (2011).

Subpress Books
Subpress is a collective that was founded by nineteen people in 1998 who donated 1% of their yearly income for six years. Each person who donated has since then had the opportunity to edit one book every three years. This book was published in the sixteenth year of the collective. It is the fourth book with Juliana Spahr as editor.

Cover and interior layout by Cassandra Smith
Cover art Redell Olsen

isbn: 1-930068-56-5

Subpress, Oakland branch is currently at 5000 MacArthur Boulevard in Oakland, California 94613.

Subpress books are distributed by Small Press Distribution.
www.spdbooks.org

“I am sending you all these details in a small drawing, so that with both the written account and the drawing you will be able to consider my wishes in this matter.”

Isabella d’Este to Pietro Perugino

"In these installations I was working with the model of an audience which is not watching a live situation at all, but the broadcast of an activity that's going on simultaneously somewhere else. Something had happened in that space in which you stand and the video functioned as a proposal for what that may or may not have been."

Matthew Barney

THE MASQVE

OF

POEMS,

TRVE DISCRIP-
tion of a

Perſonated by

WITH THE SEVERAL
Antimaſques.

OR,

Nimph.

THE LATE

VISION OF

LONDON

***PUNK FAUN:* A BAR ROCK PASTEL**

or the ***MASQUE***, *a true description: titled against*
itself: a ticker application: running text on commodity
Mini LED Display: ***personated*** with several
antimasques: *for being a true account of*
lives in ***studiolos:*** *streaming MARKET Wall interiors*
sometimes BLEAK with RÜCKENFIGURS: *Deers*
on the main road: display solutions beyond STAR
FURNISHINGS and all wildness ROCKED in
Styrene ***LADIES of Honour*** *with some ground*
UNDER *before* ***DEMALLED*** *to panel Recession,*
WHISTFUL DRIVE *towards a* **cloven poetics** *down*
Experience Economy Betwixt the acts in pastel ***GROTT*** *such*
O s *with pastoralist fancies,* ***CLUNK*** *rewind for juke*
clunk ***JUKE*** *or fast for* ***INFO WALL***
presentation by grotesque
DEVIOUS ANIMAL high bids
got up in BROCADE.

curtains as setting out

irksome in conditions close
to buying in spite of audit
subcontract to down pin only
in receipt of authentic whine
you desire cheerful from
present duty to sell up and
read on so I humble tender
happiness multi-blessed in
governing statistics never
so rich in your possessions
debit all mind pledges to
charity altered for my oblation
or a phone in caring for
entertainment graphs bare all
stuffed with Bambi saddled
for war a complete set of
benefits for mechanical larynx
sings hemp and bamboos
bite the sweat making treads
in trend that keeps the rural
retreat in the new city centre
peachy tweets artful business
obliges loyalty beside the
humblest squeals of interest
your fair share in honourers

from the capitals of every pilaster
a strange music of wild instruments
scene divided into two parts from the roof to the floor
the consorts both sound again
as one amazed speaks
pages return toward the scene
while this cloud was vanishing the wood being the under-part of the scene
was insensibly changed
in place thereof appeared four of silver
the first order consists of all gold, set with rubies, sapphires, emeralds, opals
and such like
the capitals were composed and of new invention
over this was a bastard order with cartouches reversed
the upper part rich and full of ornament
full song supported now by clouds
their arms converted into scrolls
under their waists a foliage and other carvings
bore up an architrave from which was raised a light covering arched
interwoven with branches through which the sky beyond was seen
their habits were mixed between ancient and modern
shoulders trimmed with knots of pure silver
in the upper parts where any earth could fasten were some strange forms
so high as the top pierced the clouds
the chorus of the beloved people came forth
led by Concord and the Good Genius of Great Britain
their habits being various

they go up to the state and sing

opening as a curtain of artificial sea flows itself abroad tinned aisles
sails on pop soup storm blankets thrown to arms with polymer smile

their cults were spoken of wherever there were cans

fleet of foot calorific numerologists compare motives in daily fix-up
in jest hieroglyphics Elvis Liz Marilyn condensed in mute packaging

sky—only not as recess—walking as on flats of—colour deployed
then across—whole cylinders attract—float—arms—becoming
branches—surprise lack—an admission of a reached ledge
shoulders sprout—whole lift—trees or sky in
retreat—shapes made river—pencil clouds
marked—play lines at bodies—float weight
arms branch—above clasp—breeze takes reach
of lead–

gildings owed custom branded labels for bottled water all covered camera
free speech by numbers in interests of a fair gamble and easy wipe thrones

their cults were spoken of wherever there were ads

lifted from a birds eye view frozen moons chicken winged charioteers free
range fans inscribed names merged at chocolate fountain of domestic lip

skin barks against sky—pains waking—static no longer—goes
ploy of figuring—tackle to bring down—stats of limbs in flight cannot
hold so gives—twig tress—entwining legs—ledge in inked
sky—the balletic hop—where the weight is clasp
to arms—call becoming out as branch graze
pixel beyond skirts—cursor at cupid click—insert
pale for back—lines equal horizons—the ledge
as a screen

demographics of personalised pop-ups gone global in the run up
to requisite blankness bespoke mailers who do the epistolary lick

their cuts were spoken of wherever there were candies

service splendours joined forever in the decoration of a house price
or going public in the lobby with a shared plaque above the bench

yellow is for distance—sky only backs out—a flat wept in area
a ballet clasp over one—an arm wrench—the weight is hurt
weight is blue or is a dress—cannot hold lives—edge tears
ledgewise to under

pink specs for human—gold for fur—sky clog
varnish—blue distains back—dress of bunching
an admission marks—eyes down—branch harms
figures certain in drapery—lodge hold

small wax models define the musculature of attitudes struck
someone nearby looks up pertinent actions attempts escape

or accepts confinement in an ideal plaster écorche with lids
a foreshortened future in a stripped monochrome drips up

against gravitational pull or manners an easily recognised
pout stylish beside itself flaying gestures ornate to ceiling

Stubbs sticks to horses envious as a Real Work of Art trots
by and the sinews wilt among materially assumed set ups

and learned behaviours that bring flesh upon you by the
book unleashed incite and overturn battered to a cod-face

or found floating in vats of abstraction all flap anatomy
and fugitive sheets hidden beneath emotional zones mapped

and covered by the skin of public transports an anatomical
study of the swooning virgin supported by two holy women

takes the escalator in search of famous states-of-mind districts
and is disappointed by the lack of opportunities for concrete

interventions there is the use of ropes and pulleys for support
in tiring or difficult poses, the classical lycra sheen body that

opens with a hinge is set on silent mode so as not to disturb
those in the bleachers worried about missing a single strike

variants marked points of

x   x

flaked anti-shaman shaman shows

woman in gold bearing megaphone

a struggle to mutate only satisfies

against what resists while moving

                    x

swathed in felt isolate insulate see

                       x

nothing of the soil on a blackboard

flanked   show of feeling   soul / sold

x

athletic surpass of threshold after

x

each limit set consumed as orb

all raging spot-lit to chin at desk

silver swim suit under bath-robe

x

strokes a toy stuffed deer now

a dead hare would be unkind

aesthetic   object   fond one

girl-satyrs mermaids showgirls

x

under lab coats feathers bulge

x

too many clothes rather than art

too few gestures as the chorus line

x

shopping channel pocket mirrors

x

to cheque appearance frequents

fearsome   act   planting apparent

evidence filters to point scalp

x x

as use towards prosthetic ears

with hidden noise engraves

two copper plates four bolts

enclose a ball of twine around

x x

an unseen object that rattles

treated fears objection reason is

x

when shaken insert by a friend

x

with complaints against perfect

plasticity or volume evidence

of decline in vocal sound as if

x

proximity the only subjective

x

possibility not I was ere I was

pack connector subject error

x

listening elsewhere in surround

to what might never be happens

possessing by possession anyway

x x

this thing talking machine records

x

how far this mute record moves from

its object and is allowed to proceed

listing sample recollects reckoning

snares for silence in required voice

snares for silence

snares for noise

exclude welcome

welcome excludes

against its own

own extreme falls

if unfettered her
voice requires

bodies rendered
needy incomplete

only the problem
reproduction not

that what is heard
apparently must be

seen throwing its
trembling body

forward quaint
if flesh speaks

true how dull
herrings make

a machine for
right process

sounds differently
exceeds comfort

not finding voice
nature but noising

tidal disputes
silence interrupts

its noisy self
a walk on bit

already given
understudies

pay for what
doing feels like

blocks jogged
search to track

chorus of modular units

light of adhesive squint beyond the market in art toss
yeah right or think other side the big capital P posed

by He who struts in grim mechanical feet presents
cowboy heels as rich ornament or encloses placards

MAKE IT YOUR WAY IN PREPREPARED MODULAR UNITS
pre-fab come grammar or cannot imagine my suppose to

raises the perceived stakes stiff upper lip so brand identikits
great branches cluster orientated merchandise leaves to husk

corniced INTERACTION WITH BOLD AND HELPFUL STUFF
dressed as mergals or car mechanics or beauty counters make

scallops shaped by sponsors inside high ride distortion subjects
popcornied through virtual networks spangles no spitting here

miked up to tannoy masses read on ric rac my flounce spruce up
concern go proceed to hemp yourselves shopping as air shirts

get poisonous plastic oblige seals beside of humblest honourers
pin loyalty badge to small pressed community butts swill in wonder

ATTENTION SHAPERS COIN a rollator awaits in the mist is placed a large compartment composed of grotesque work neon fauns attend on bespoke READY TO WEARY situationist distractions lurk disnified to protect the food court in oil use the buttons on the left to find the best way for transports sake keep booming the hub steads with another solution in search of non-combatants or insurgents one bagged to indifference cue pathetic fanfare of ears cocked prosthetic daily glossies delay as an ally sips champagne in the new nail gun and lounge cordon and kicked off air to ground soft on target

of ceilings

two breathe clouds across the sky to one another
being scarred by birds they stand on wavy air
push on neighbouring particles to make tunes I
permanently bound into the stuff of naked walls
slaked lime paste and coarse marble on canapés
between points of compression the china bones
as see through this longitudinal nicety gasps up
tempo as do I I do resounds over shelves rusty
in casting shapely hearts or how the head holds
a flood marker gauges stubborn wet lime marked
in place of face grinds pigment for speaking out
of rheuming it through violently spun air blubbers
a funnel for listening with what cannot be fanfare
stronger for liquid intake concrete quibbles stick
but in itself does not vibrate stocks of the same
if all surfaces are magnets then we might travel
cheaply outside to find ourselves encrusted at
the navel with the body of a man or the torso of
a horse and buy it up in expectation of the pain
in kick that is deployed as a mammal might be

in enemy waters where even dolphins have teeth
pulling away fast from what look like shells AWOL
or just meeting up with the other local marine life
to search for patterns at every nth click tears
past Standard Gas Stations gestations in series
painted in black and orange L'AMOUR or L=I=S=P
spelled out in ribbons rime can be thick enough
to resemble shades enchanted for repel of damage

chorus in demonstration mode

in demonstration mode behind a table filled with root vegetables
today an offering of forty per cent or more of gross leasable area

as hard intelligence little inconvenience to the hosts of rock throwers
later exploded by ordnance alight to the glare of white phosphorus

fizz broken frontispiece wrought with scrolls mask heads of children
we up drive on a plinth to the recreation of the centre a vase of gold

flourish smart card reader cuts frequency of visits as plotted by a giraffe
complete with fruitages or hangings disabled for permanent access

live at the foot of a mystery shopper two Shebeg Shepherds alongside
and their dog a Loughtan ram all in their natural poetry colours

hurry as stocks limp damaged banners drape FUN AND ENJOYABLE
poppy eradication tours ringed with coils of razor wire flag ripples

disposable dailies

designed for everyday life but mostly out of range
between various small fires nightly on TV a dog
chews a skirt and a scooter carries a bucket of
water as a chariot carries a peacock to a jolly good
show at the arthouse battery while a midriffed
attack bluffs an achingly breathless feat driving
a transit van freeway GALATEA rolling out of lanes
into a dark blue sky permanently lost in gold plate
tossed out after the main course into the Tiber
sights for a banked sore eye in mock tapestry
gone with the job of painting in the curtains or
straddling forced cirrus and falling from tromped
oils done neatly ice effect grates for furnishing
reflections in the droplets just like a real life
wrestle with a lion or an ally or a landscape hidden
in a wall your breast is at an angle as if slipped
off by some cumulous translation as restoration
of a fixed point from which to survey an imaginary
view from around the back as some future watcher
positioned cornered up walls garlanded outlandish
with plants just discovered happily already there

stars bid

stars bid last orders long before
gilded chrysler's day cabs new
alloy of fear the glory axel slays

foes mincing goals for heavenly
accessory usury of must-haves
slouchy flats prowling print of

pert fairies snag lycra forms in
closer to Rome trimmings travel
lonely flowers caved in hearts

rose braided twines a pochette
budget covets trends quivered
Girl-Satyrs go alight machine slots

rowing all harboured to step
stations yogic purity testifies
sharing arms or jacuzzi times

soulesss gels clothed shacks
contagion slinky free radicals
recall the pride of after care

ghouls chamber paces blood
counters plumping gloss got
E-6 Mercury stud details chic

cover-boy liquid remembers
clarity even patriotic smiles
to gives proof of off the peg

tattoo or love's new slight
failing graceful on fat free
a C-130 Hercules monitors

visually lifts the corners eyes
work this trend for coloured
shoeboots on wood Girl-Satyrs

decking go bar rock all for
fingers down throats to trim
later Hail Goddess of Wash

gulp amphibious assaults
phalanx of ten spets her glob
thickest turns all seeing stony

in kill game embroidered vale
violence of feeders polluted
Come Queen of Muzak a blot

on enhanced contours Come
nail bar hands beat the ground
in a light Campari round this

plasma blister jollity in dance
of armoured personals of airy
shells of emergent fiery clouds

of scrambling net enhanced
chrones clad plastic face off
pixel caress in cabled nook

diagrams of tubular refashioning

i.

a like composition varies figures oval on top
bourne up by eatertainment impressa develops

property or a baby sprouting plastic flowers
ten pound notes and three lesser coins spring

out of the stems lined with MORE THAN JUST
A PLACE SELLING GOODS AND MERCHANDISE

heads shape a scroll for Fifties hostess honey maker
factors mass scares volume adverts for a stronger eye

maxi fright doors show essential black out vanity casing
ever long massing high tech application to soft warning

I wand is eye curling in the world weighed lids did this
I did that hoops as I wound her cornet through thinking

choke on this how to develop a word for spokes wound
second time and found it as a blushing powder blown

ii.

wise column circled inches
over suspense by airy truss
night stubs mass sleepless
on tofu dream luv scrapes

rosy triumphs on metered
voltage or growth in civic
chivalry real tv out flounces
demure as starved twiglets

thirsty on gal-glossed pints
blue-eyed in contacts teary
as oh ah sauce buttons slip
out spies another polyester

his throws suffer chalet style
loan playing the catalogue
loot loaded bleep on base
lines inspiration lacks rock

against huge hype of sky
retro fringes frame calmed
secrets intimate envy stars
sunbed fresh satyrs trance

pinky hued across pattern
couched infants drunk on
fuelled tenderness blankly
come down in pop shades

slumbering Antiope drags
on as some Jupiter paws
the furnishings upstairs a
nereid takes it all in cold

showers rushes of hollow
din infesting walls in sob
guilty potions priced up
weak wan of purging sale

iii.

newest and most gracious all this lip ornament tat
this palace of fasteners and brushed maple sheen
these carved accents spoken as overlay mouldings
tanned hide of added historical importance bloats
impressive with amount of holy media stored within
or worn from day to night as a ruffle on a little stick
memories fobbed off by utterances rams keen home

iv.

in city pastille turns a
moving field of pauses
facts shunted through
de luxe knowing panes

gamely look throughs
wary of lyric tendons
fused serpent angelic
figures as statues read

standing clouds of flat
planes diagrammatic us
alcoves of spaces not
not scheming for depth

regurgitate navigations
some may knowingly
appear twice in pinks
of drapery in the same

panel before and after
happens as uncreases
simultaneous in sense
of overlay but able to

occur jointly on plain
surface other scales of
such multiple ordering
faces blew crowds on

v.

fire curtain flying up on the sudden hand crafted
shape desired behaviour total demographic friendly

discovered the scene represents authenticity
kin air looms three parts of crotch mahogany

boasts a lovely patina physically distressed even
just lack of sleep worn at edges eyes worm holes

heaps of safety temper tantrums arched glass
door features lower storage fittings patented TWIST

-LOCK handles statues lying as if complete assembly
needed 66 cardboard case VHS tapes 56 oversized

256 DVDs or 328 CDs are the ruins of some great city
or ancient dictatorship LOVE IS FULL OF HISTORY WITH

ALL THE VERSATILITY OF HOW WE LIVE TODAY
is neon for singles or those lifted out to room alone

vi.

heroic awnings spread homey over patios owed
echoes through nappy leisure land lamby snack
stained exes dribble buns made kids left folded
naked on these our dashing flints still measuring

big by things of loss torn coin pockets bushels
of green thongs braced in building heart cans
imperative territory in alteration conversion lofts
bulls to stud at the coax school points to bullet

toxic honey sulks at the thought of foreign bees
branded flocks of possessions makes man made
in other words how rich I am in showy milk see
I drive the stag with a green marshmallow stick

lovely mug of youth Girl-Satyrs a laden clutch off
with spokes up Brick Lane pale irises to sell tolls
of self rugwised come past bleach emote my tat
clinched in severance ready splayed insurance

laurels counted in forms of bleak ink a note to
lovers of happy times some cult is beckoning
with promise of empty so Go Goatherds Go
Faithful as a bendy Narcissus poses a strike

and holds Go wary Poppy-Headers of settees
read pipes wax joined not in name but living
in singeing years of takings i.e. no more a
stranger to my dogs than the moon herself

mark rented tree-tops where doves have built
on brown fields udders corporation feathered
cash flowers gather in bladdered meadows to
kiss the packaging panic-grass stems of wound

lonely landfill lies licking hurry for bleak high
as energy banks juice up carboniferous eras
withdrawn biomass pay back timed squeaky
exploits of energy efficient forest certification

songs of woodland tryst spoils appeal to mass
locked-in darkly then subjected to loud music
gifts lavished by fee empires roaming foxes
prowling gloved around city wails of schemed

assistance rife volunteering returns of energy
needs willow coppice mildewed grain chicken
litter and sewage sludge a significant provision
to slay this age not late in competition metals

the celebration of who were the celebrators

for YOU the English licks of lineage upgrown American and shiny come homey bright glorious plasma twins of RECS and UECS before whose throne refined blend of lovelies in aged patina drive up frequency for YOUR bespoke bar rock targets for YOU who also carry home theater options and for YOU who do not require a stand to shed joy with safety glass for YOU whose hearts beep for manufacture for YOU who provide free support upon receipt or fresh from toll for YOU who fix displays of blah or brandings and for YOU at edutainment auditions for YOU not sworn off surfers in antic whine

noise minds mechanical

disturbed off cuts of chat

noise minds mechanical

oratory branch

corals
mouth

open proper

hole go express up

gesture sky swallows defectors

join crystal tears in total stain well *sluggin*
of weeps engrave the stone vial *tubular*
music for tank rides join hurl down *whatever*
on goths bled lips splayed global fur *go postal*
currency made in deodands *fer shur*
monumental as shaped chews *don't have a cow*
balsam spits gum up blob precious *leave it out*
or gag with porcelain spooning in *utter barf*
valley girl loves punkess in glew *far out*
go trip and print them up roses *wicked*
hunt with slain justice mostly saved *like totally*
in Girl-Satyrenburg milk and sugar *grody to the max*
dyed fingers bold cottoned charm *on sweet*
wounded in high rise terminal *duh*

at banners

COME ON
YOU NYMPHS
FAUN STRATEGIC

FEELING FLOODS
FLOODS
FEELING

OH
DOLLOP
OH

WADS BARGE
IN GUSH

GRAZE
DEEPS
WITH
TRUSTY
NAVEL

SPRIGHTLY
NEEDS
FROWN
NOW
IN PLASTIC

PROW

ROW

ROW

PRO

CRYING SHAMED
FEATURES

RUN
WATERY
RUIN

PANDAEYESME

GO
SATYR GO
LITHE GO
HONESTLY GO

DOWN REAL

TEARS OPENLY

[SHE]

Come with our vices let us war
  Anus-island of hulk
Screen tested drones unite us now
  And all is turned death metal

[HE]

So clear Big Ben is in the lap
 While Chrysler punks above
An oily truth of nature in excess
 Triumphant blast of will

[SHE]

O wail of orifice and torture
  Ornaments to heal crowds
O karaoke me the scrimmage
  Tourist trophies of the kill

[HE]

What preservation shouts hang on
  Highest rung of gilded hands?
O faerie isle what colour sounds
  Like caprification state?

[SHE]

Idyllic shepherd of modern
  Man fascinate me your arms
Clasping the dead dailies to us
  And call innocence a blush

[HE]

Deskbound eager for evil tastes
  Castration rodeo TV
What hurls itself into the mosh?
  We want the sting that words

as performed in our own person

in homage to the cupids in Domenichino's *The Assumption of Mary Magdalen into Heaven*, 1617-1621, I will ascend the escalator at Waterloo Station wearing a wing shaped ruff fashioned from today's newspaper.

in homage to Francesco Albani's *Toilet of Venus* c. 1620 I will hire an assistant (living wage) to push my child and I around the Grand Arcade shopping mall. We will wear uniforms of blue gowns embroidered with stars and sourced from female workers in Vietnam. I will breastfeed while reapplying lipstick in every available shop window.

in homage to *Portrait of a Man Holding a Medallion of Cosimo Medici* (c. 1474/75) by Sandro Botticelli I will hammer 100 chocolate coins into a newly upholstered red velvet sofa.

in homage to Luca Giordano's *The Fall of The Rebel Angels* (1666) I will jog on a specially designed running machine while chanting "Down With The Rebels" until I fall down from exhaustion. I will be wearing a blue tracksuit, gold trainers and carrying a coffee cup branded to match the tattoo of the bare breasted siren on my right hand. If commissioned to make this piece for Saudi Arabia, I will remove the siren, leaving only her crown. The power generated by my run will be available as a limited edition of units for any members of the audience to purchase at a reduced market rate and suitable for a variety of domestic applications.

a slide show primer (on behalf of the warden)

This is of a chord sprinkled thicket
This is of a diagram which proves it
This is of a footnote that explains what pancakes are
This is of a perpetual fear of those on the outside whose job it is to grid the
  internals
This is of a pure flank
This is of a shape that is not always an innocent container
This is of a softening into flesh and blood from something else
This is of a tufted slumber
This is of an abstract thing or it might be a nipple
This is of an ear as it would be seen inflating from inside the body
This is of artificial breath
This is of a caudal appendage or so-called tethered form
This is of imported seedless gapes
This is of not just human
This is of nothings purring
This is of nylon and how it suspends many small things that would otherwise
  be falling

This is of one laughing as an expression of foolishness
This is of one laughing who does not appear to be expressing anything
This is of one of those funny pink things Eva Hesse made before she went
  grey
This is of one rollerblading through an airport
This is of one that is like some string coiled up
This is of one weeping as an expression of ecstasy
This is of one weeping who does not appear to be expressing anything
This is of one which is quite like the sign nearby that says not to
This is of one which might have been used as a squeaker for a small dog
This is of signals from a kept live and natural wild wild
This is of some ears with pointed ends
This is of some safety pins which were used to keep it together
This is of some string coiled up
This is of some verbal wallpaper as was vetoed by the warden
This is of the fur in transit and still breathing
This is of the heart of the timid
This is of the increase through the perforation and damage

This is of the long yellow ropes that were used
This is of the other side of the scaffolding as Clovis saw it
This is of the place where it was found to be punctured
This is of the same consistency as the resin that clogged the interior and
  made it difficult to say anything
This is of the she-wolf suckling
This is of the taxi driver with paws or maybe they were just gloves
his is of the way the joke was found face down in a lay-by past caring
This is of tresses knotted in horns
This is of use within properly prescribed limits

PATRONSOFPOETICINVENTIONDEMAND

some swimming through the river
some flying
some riding upon white swans

ballet snares industrielle

in lair   snare

wares   beware

a glade is burst[1]
a holiday floors

the pleasants[2]
faints at feats

---

[1] Air indicates one in movement as off is visible and strung. A working being on leggy grind. Toe to hip to head at hyper zoom. Learn the vocabulary of the machines to communicate with operators whole. Verb directional hit.

[2] Alms in pixelated banners float. A market for riots online auctioned. Collectors mass whole inside slouch to engine. Dances with excavators.

entonic lunge

lawn passes
sparse of fray

as worn in forklift ballet flats lost machinicity conduction

warm in swarm

a meadow near the castle cedes asks
a momentary hallucination halation

plate

that fragile is
a rate of beats
that ends her[3]

chain a

a return to hunt

a swan comes out of the lake and into a girl

a transformation of wings or arms
a true form reminiscent of a bird

a word is torn for[4]

---

[3] Ball-like or the bouncing step of two robots. A step in which springs various orders. Occasional collisions between individuals of certified types. The grid was filled with test tubes for online facings. Rank air extends one leg to the front, side or back and lands start in history. The tottering is feudal. A system for self-manufacture extends the leg towards either class. May be executed in all the directions of the body which can be programmed elsewhere.

[4] New produces an exchange of chains, links like prosthetic devices for virtual feeling inc. This is an abbreviation of the term for a series of rapid turns on the points done in a straight line or in a circle. Rapid developments across tabs now closing.

darn sea crack tether

an allowance human becomes as ether

and turns into another
approaches dawn

assures it of no harm and steps out[5]

say O sway away face

[5] Any national or folk dance, or a dance based on movements associated with a particular profession, trade, personality or mode of living. The rise of steam. Commune was the name taken for ease of marketing to those familiar with luxury.

by night is only a human thing[6]

dies of broken faces sway
disappears and slips away

distance is
measured by
horns sounding
give tally

evidence that the peasant is not[7]

fanfares announce arrivals
forest of ones not unlike her

emerges with a word and says so sword

---

[6] Shaded in place of old wants. One is burst asunder and the word proceeds to checkout. Adopts a stance at an oblique angle to the banner. A part is taken aback and almost hidden. Virtual overlays of light. Lost from view despite the reach towards an invisible commercial.

[7] Now open, now hidden. This direction is termed as a verb or as a method. Faces used to qualify a pose in which the legs are open and not crossed out. A prose taken as deviant or demure. What is a mere instrument of production? Codes for ethics ragged in borrowed costumes left on the step for collection.

pole sawn

he instinctively reaches for his words

(which as a nobleman he is
  accustomed to

presents him with a bow

lake of mother's tears
one is hastily departing[8]

---

[8] The heavy artillery to batter down walls is a literary barb carried aloft. Glide. A traveling step executed by the glide of the working foot from the fifth position through its exploitation by global fibs. My doll is a system of taxation. Counts me in. Produces and consumes in every country in the required direction. A city break. Another foot closing. *Glissade.* The weight is shifted to the working foot with a *fondu* to the use of machinery. The other foot, pointed a few inches from the floor, slides into the fifth position in *demi-plié.* There is an estate agent of propriety outside awaiting a curtsey.

of stricken influence

probability that that is not the real shape of it[9]

proceeds to another shape[10]

refreshments are served to the hunters

release seems certain

some hours later enters to hunt

swan-maidens made anxious by disappearances[11]

swans in flight mood slip

swears to be her always

---

[9] When a *glissade* is used as an auxiliary step for small or big jumps, it is done with a quick movement on the upbeat conditions by which they are fettered. *Glissades* are done with or without a change of feet, and all begin and end with a *demi-plié*. She becomes an appendage of the machine: *devant, derrière, dessus, en avant.* Measures the difference between them as well as the direction taken towards pay. *Glissade* may also be done *sur les pointes*, exacted in a given time or by increasing speed of her connection from home.

[10] Large *jeté* forward. A big leap forward preceded by a preliminary movement such as a *pas couru* or a *glissade*, which gives the necessary push-off. Constant revolutionising of production, uninterrupted disturbance of all social conditions, everlasting uninterrupted disturbance of all social conditions, *everlasting* uncertainty and agitation.

[11] The jump is done on the foot which is thrown forward as in *grand battement* or atoms of information at ninety degrees. The height of the jump depends on virtual and ceaseless product. The length of the jump depending on the strong push-off of the other increasing speed and the decreasing of costs far away.

that the gold necklace is not a sign keeping
the black swan is radiant
the body of him who must be protected[12]
the dance is to stop it happening
the destiny of change
the forest shields them

the passion of a cross bow
the shock of duplicity[13]
the spell of

the traditional test is with a daisy

---

[12] She tries to remain in the air in a definitely expressed attitude to out sourcing, or as an *arabesque* towards the removal of workers from the balance sheet. It is important to start the jump with a springy *plié* and finish it with a soft and controlled electronic sign to be remediated presently. Nestled and settled everywhere.

[13] Line. The outline scanned by one while executing steps and poses. Sense of line according to the arrangement of head, body, legs and arms in a pose or movement as of seen on a chip. Lost in gaussian blur. Forged the weapons that bring death to itself, call into existence the dancers who are to wield themselves as weapons by remote.

to live spelling breaking

to vengefully trap a shade

rest is none and moving[14]

Tour en l'air

wares   beware

snare   in lair

[14] Circular. A term applied to steps or *enchainments* executed in a circle. The burden of toil.

villagers pass by on their way to harvest the grapes[15]

[15] Turn in the air. Gives radical rupture. Arms assist and the head must spot. A mere training to act as a machine or a turn in the air as virtual one. The dancer rises straight into the air from a *demi-plié* makes a complete turn and lands in the fifth position with the feet reversed. The turn may be single, double or triple according to the permissions granted. May also be finished in various poses such as attitude, *arabesque* or on one knee. May be done in series against the music sounded.

barriers at map

i.

maps memorise the invisible
fence around general saunter
remembers the wall in the head
once deadly borders now nested
song birds occupy forgotten how
for them no space of patterns gone
disrupts erstwhile barriers while
cross lynx howls up watchtowers
absorbs where ends once stalked
met what cat calls a Free Whorl
red while deer trail traditional
lies now wild with GPS receivers
reports that she cannot cross
what mothers established then
yellow collars report wearers
location blocs to avoid conflict
data dots a stubborn refusal
blinking on electronic leash
memorise the invisible maps
fenced for general slaughter

ii.

it restrains beyond buildings move
flesh does hues of slobbery unfold

scalings I shrink impinges classical
skits how feebles it dross for yowl

earnest pom pom an oval bursts at
vista te daaa lone obstacle I blinks

thrown across isle of raging teats
furniture slippery in its unwonted

street curve ne nah ne nah columns
boss to con squeal jokes a distance

facades riddled with holes conceal
documents that propose what might

have been a decor of painted skies
at eye-level in contradistinction to

floor protruding cornices the tags are
set for mild vertigo clumping room

after vroom vroom disjoining just
bleep to send through stacked roles

missing foreground the edge over
ran diagonal weather inspires none

but plastic as marble or gold as fluid
invisible as money as solidity springs

a leaky mass or a spear bigger than
a pine on a mountain inside a glass

trained on the piercing moon St Teresa
crying in the same stone that she is rigid

not hypnotic in two kinds of drapery
repel by love for froth in good stucco

charge fixes to beat all motion all slurp
regular pangs for pain clearance rung

people

loaded dust ear

laying

arms mark roam

machine

fun dust guns

speakers

tear city bones

sound

miss skin bikini

pink

a hide for setting

an animal in general
as opposed   to human

being what   distinctions

gather in gasps

breathe

someone saw one puncture a wellington
boot on a particular frequency broadcasts
the stretch and shot placement to explore
how fast they moved through at dusk
no telephones answering live call-in shows
no reality tapes this sound is only this sound
emits a high pitch activates culture for deer
warning thereby defines a particular series
or zone of the roadway by gifting marks
its own sound signature barking
spelt damage

hearts drive
by heroes   rot

passage works   site

sylvan
slivers

spaces

by passing

through
aural topiary

moving

is listening through

reaches

a destination

whistle heard above traffic in velvet
over-familiar threatens secure in use
seven radio transmitters activate headlights
strobe drove at overlap through zone
material picked up mixed by speed
location and trajectory startles to stop
tracks as vehicles pass safely on every
life bolstered in material certainty devices
machines daily assembled in 1966
for themselves
only inside

is listening in

on an inside

a static sound structure set into

motion

thought
falls within

this vector

noise alert

passing through noise tuning specific
adjustments towards effects at present making
stag shift to become ones own musical performance
already tests run to determine how they tend
to delay crossing longer after traffic has passed
until such devices establish sonic horizons known
a noise to them active in the phrasing of day
a static sound gives way with use plural same
name badgers are protected and cannot be
culled reaction to the art elicited differs
either species
to species

just deterrents

if cornered on the part

of listeners
who cannot
judge increasing

roads roaming

new acoustic devices found fondness

emits high frequency

in warning

numbness

territory defined as cars

speed claim sounds

mixing the direction

dogs attacked even

aggressive empty

vessels make most

to avoid in urban

move live from location to sound

background traps

feed with assault

into motion noise

locale structures of motion
pass
environmental

what weathers are
conditions of matter dry
swerving
as a consequence
of impact

how far to the left
or right side of unlike

originals from original

or around recorded keeps deer off

depends on   from

which direction   one enters

for those   who love   to rock out

                        in public places   with headphones

the grassy pieces   councils can cull
in long leafy   roads tended   in phases   or

GOT TO REMEMBER   installed   at 50m

live intervals   against   harm

for songs at tongue

i.

drawn in by ravished melody
her fault of homeliness a pick
willing to endure low cushions

entertained on progresses out
to get milk we have run out of
questions or what queen dances

best not to be outdone in duties
so stole the pose from paintings
in strict meter where is the song

in that dancing the volta again
only the dog has moved laps
masquers make entry on the stairs

besydes musycke and syngynge
we commuters hum inside spaces
blindly open to the world bars or

little flexi paires of iron brackets
to set up divers exquisite authors
six or seven gallyards in mornynge

an instruction to bring into action
lungs or fingers Vertical axis read
as chords mouthings up escalators

wood cased words hiss as moulds
protection for heat open as hinges
personal molten type-metals struck

by punches bearing intimate slogans
abrasive as labels down shirt backs
signets on the strip of rawness some

decorative initials added in colour
hands note taken ready to market
uneasy watching slides to pocket

audible movements one hundred
times smaller than the diameter
of atoms hydrogen kissed at hiss

of rumor heard of as a grotesque
she was a small space filled with
mute matter out cries prevent just

such dissipation the calorie quota
for roaring out of shot reaches at
tongue to voice a pricked ear loud

as icing congeals as word clouds
this city of woulds melts later only
so much breath wasted without noise

ii.

signals arising from the test setup

invite flung and dragged as eye

droppers train on ice water steam

sound drip pour out towards event

leaks past objects flee whole with

utter shrug off fixity as occasional

moments going piped burst open

as panting tight lipped at closed

avoid flood limits gross with feelers

fallers transmit position swatches
matter going minimised as reflection
fancy radiation shields structure

the test equipment as opposed to
the equipment under test givens
without hope dress up in wooden

and plastic things a full-scale spoon
or at least a life-size representation
sold as seen one chamber once lined

not normally permitted inside rises
high gain to the point of combustion
tells it like it is like it is telling it like

a recording for defunct ears devoid
of conduct transfer discharge within
a range of perforations use as filters

a screen room traps random person
risk assessment posed by spurious
transducers in pursuit of pure tone

iii.

head down ready to attack   domesticates
noise from wild these decoys sweep reliability
what wolf puts up his parka hood   stars

two imitate the silhouette   one floored
stage-struck shout   lifts her bow or gun as antlers
drawn   it will approach

correctly   to live them out in face
splayed out   how not to be physical about that
strip danceable utterly   or avoid all humans

rejoin their own speech herd   riffs struggle
up day-glo   snares in human form
alarmed at   neat fringe of hiding

as do-it-yourself tough   just a persona found
protruding from a vulva-shaped crack in a tree
birthed this familiar yawn   velveteen girls

pale   what no single word covers
swept   away tame marked by stones reindeer carved
beyond map space   slits   historical

I give you the naturally made-up   disgust me
or look for something else   say this goo sticks
they can't play   is part tattoo

for ink stylizes movement   from function
towards legend and never seen   unsteady vocal
sounds defect ear plugged detachment   she

xeroxed lyrical   demands migrations
explores try out returns as European or
American Rudolf invented by advertising

copywriter 1939   gifted economies
wrapping stone and skin in the same impulse   surface
connections   not erratically wandered

between this shape and an after-life
hunting for a copiest of the first Raincoats album
thinks of her sprouting motifs instead

or lying in a parker protected from sums
net hem unravelling   organic does not
remain unthreatened makes mention of

how she discovered that the milk was off
rolls a trumpet out of birch bark   hip to spit
out more wordings of the cost price

imitates strong wailing available in English
counting the pack animals before they are ridden
some distance from bar rock and pastel

in hot-pink heel on a shoe hat worn
by an heiress   shades who risk travel to the sun
and back on a flying one tipped

with birds   each one passed around
fire of identical lines razored or hairy aqua netted
earmarks of a developing statement

of fishnets and combats against dippy
to brassy *guerre des robes*   younger girls passing
out phasers   in orange and fuschia gold

what commitment fashions as opt
out soon harvested   shifts waiver on seams
billed as vehicles of quick release

The 16th Song.

put some thrash on and stuff your piney whispers

of days spent pasturing
ready-made containers
boxed lap-tips control
snacks chemise finalists
on hands free daytime
stuff my rented cup
floods o'er basement
patent winners hum
floral etch-a-sketch
rims of murky family
wax ornamental dry
instant crystal self goo

put some thrash on and stuff your piney whispers

two-handled so goods
at being in the queue
newly made of tinned
fresh out still chemical
works keeps on at use
less spoils counter sell
beans policy grow suck
swollen after fall pouts
back to task imagines
train for desk bound
bleach marvels strike
quip roots from Hades

put some thrash on and stuff your piney whispers

touch feeling marks as
stone a groove known
of metals cash or piss
factory *ahhs* for sonic
reducers of nightingale
wafting lean on blast
hearty mind of karaoke
anxious for cultivates
dead good in plastic
plants tonight I aim
bucolic is overheard
not born a billy-goat

put some thrash on and stuff your piney whispers

fed future bleeps up
demographic shapes
hides of mutual calf
yoked pod celebrants
kiss competitors goth
products in hair spill
libations aisle slick
lips rung from shot
age shred pack info
skins echo plasma
kids eaten alive tax
estate granted bleats

put some thrash on and stuff your piney whispers

songs at locked doors
out disobey certainties
matter resists matter
let collagen improve
piping let the mouse
taste the pitch let out
for the split-oops voice
or belly-crawl let's off
give snort to the peck
let's move to pieces
let's lay in sheaves of
office stationery ground

F I N I S.

ADVERTISEMENTS.

There is now published,

Redell Olsen's previous publications include: 'Book of the Fur' (Rempress, 2000), 'Secure Portable Space' (Reality Street, 2004) and the collaboratively edited bookwork 'Here Are My Instructions' (Gefn Press, 2004). From 2006 - 2010 she was the editor of *How2* the online journal for modernist and contemporary poetry, poetics and criticism by women. Her recent projects have involved texts for performance, film and site-specific collaboration and include: 'Newe Booke of Copies' (2009), 'Bucolic Picnic (or *Toile de Jouy Camouflage*)' (2009) and 'The Lost Swimming Pool' (2010). She is a reader at Royal Holloway, University of London where she is the director of the MA in Poetic Practice.